F*CK HIM2!

"GIRL HE'S PLAYING YOU"

Your Guidebook to his Playbook

By.

Nancy Beauplan

For information contact; address info@nancybcreatives.com

Book and Cover design by Nancy M. Beauplan

ISBN-13: 978-1542980302

ISBN-10: 1542980305

First Edition: January 2017

10 9 8 7 6 5 4 3 2 1

DEDICATION

I dedicate this book to Love. Once we realize we
are spiritual beings having an human experience
the pains of life seem some minuscule to the
greatness of love.

~Notes~

CONTENTS

~Notes~

ACKNOWLEDGMENTS

God is Love.

~Notes~

"ALL IS FAIR IN LOVE AND WAR

1

Introduction

All is fair in love and war
Unknown

"Your love life is not over." Those are the words I repeatedly had to say to myself just to get myself out of bed in the morning. I remember nights of feeling empty because I had no one to text goodnight to. No one to share conversations with and no one to fill me up with sweet nothings. My need to fill that void of love & affection began to grow bigger and bigger as the days went on. I needed to find another man fast, who could help me ease the pain of this broken heart and who could fill my desire for love.

Getting back into the dating scene seemed like the absolute worst. I didn't want to settle for a rebound, yet I was too scared to put my feelings out on the line for the real thing. So I had two options, one was to feel empty for the rest of my life or two, fight like hell to get better so I could find true love; a person I could share my love and life experiences with.

I got real with myself and realized I wanted the real thing. I wanted true love. So I decided to fight like hell. I took a year off from relationships so that I could rejuvenate and find myself again. I worked on healing, forgiveness, self-love, spirituality, life-purpose, and finances. I wanted to be *A-1* before I got back into the dating scene because I learned that you are what you attract. And I didn't want to attract a bum. So I did the work. Although I haven't found my life partner yet, over the years I have been blessed enough to be in relationships that were full of experiences that I have enjoyed and learned a lot of things from. I learned to have an appreciation for the dating game and all its ups, downs and roadblocks. So I wrote this book to share my experiences with you and what I have learned along the way, in hopes that it will help you find the courage to get back out there and enjoy the dating game while finding your true love.

If you haven't read my first book *"F*ck Him! Don't Be Bitter, Get Better & Make Money"* I urge you to grab it before reading this book because in that book we discuss the important things like healing and creating a vision for your life. In this book, we jump right into getting back into the dating game because if you want to find love, that's what you will have to do to find it. And don't get it twisted when I use the word "game" I know finding true love is nothing to be played with. But just follow me here for a second, I use the word "game" loosely because I like to think of dating as a sport. Finding love can be fun, but it can also be very competitive, strategic and dangerous if you are not careful. If you want to win at finding true love, you have to know how the dating game is being played. Mr. Right isn't just going to come knocking on your door asking you for marriage. And if he did how would you know how to handle it if you're still stuck, confused and unsure after your last relationship.

When you are so eager to find love again, you can easily fall into the trap of another *trifling* playa who can sense the desperation, and play you worse than the first guy who hurt you. So that's why I titled this book *"F*ck Him 2! Girl He's Playing: Your Guidebook to his Playbook"* because I want you to stay clear of those men. I don't want you to get your heartbroken again but I don't want you to go into hiding either. You deserve true love, but you have to know how to play the game in order to get it. I want you to know what you are getting yourself into and how to stay clear of the trifling men who are out to hurt you. The quest to finding love won't be perfect, and it won't be easy, but it will be worth it. There is no clear cut path to finding love again, but this book can be used as a guide to help you at least give it your best shot. I know how hard it is to give love a second chance. But please know that love didn't hurt you that guy did. So that's what I will be talking about in this book. You will learn how the game is being played and the type of men that are playing. How to set your standards high, stand your ground and get what you want of a relationship. And most importantly how to be patient, go with the flow and trust the process. This is the game of life, after all, it is to be enjoyed so don't be afraid to go for after love with full force.

I repeat, you should ONLY read this book after you have healed from the heartbreak of your last relationship. Because I want you to be tough enough to handle the bullshit that comes with dating. All is fair in love & war, and only the

strong survive at finding love &
relationships.

I discuss healing immensely in my first
book and even provide you with a
workbook journal to help you with the
healing process. You can pick up it up at
www.fvckhim.com Once you are done
healing then you can enter back into the
dating game. Nevertheless, if you have
been following me for a while and have
already read my first book, then you are
good to go and I guess it's safe to say "let
the games begin."

"EVEN A GOOD PLAYER WILL SOMEDAY BECOME THE TOY OF A BETTER PLAYER. IT'S CALLED KARMA.

2

All Men Are Players

Even a good player will someday become the toy of a better player. It's called karma.

Unknown

Just like any sport you have to know which position every man plays. You have to understand that not all of these men are looking for love & marriage like we women so naively want to think. Not from the jump at least. From my experience, I learned that they are 3 groups of men that are playing in the dating game. And the crazy part is each group of these men are playing the game but with different intentions.

Here goes the group of men as follows, *the Benchwarmers, the Playas, & the Starters.* They all have different intentions when entering the dating game and should be dealt with accordingly. So let's break it down.

First, you have *the* ***Benchwarmers***. These group of men are in the dating game just to score as many "points" as possible. Translation, these men want sex. They are the "hit it and quit it" type of fellas. They are not looking to be tied down to one *"team"* They are usually new to the game and very immature when it comes to relationships. Don't get me wrong, all men want sex. But the benchwarmers "ONLY" want sex. They can come off as complete assholes & douche bags because they want one thing and one thing only. And once they get it they are on to the next chick.

They start ignoring you and go missing in action. You usually find boys playing this game but unfortunately some of these boys never mature, and you find some grown men still playing with this intention. They enjoy scoring points and will not slow down until scoring points just isn't exciting anymore.

Which brings me to the next group of men, *the **Playas***. Now the *Playas* are a bit more experienced than the *Benchwarmers*. They have done a lot of "scoring" and are now looking to go after something a little bit more intense. These Playas like to play for trophies.

Let me explain, these Playas only want the MVP award. The trophy you get for being the most *vulnerable* playa. Because that's exactly what these men are, weak & insecure. *He* can be described as a heartbreaker, manipulator or narcissist, because he isn't playing for the victory of the team, he is playing for his own, individual, selfish desires. A *Playa* gets off on making girls fall in love with him and collecting their hearts as trophies. Once he has gotten a girl's heart he usually breaks it because he is too busy trying to win the heart of another girl, you know to keep the excitement of the game going. Often times if you get into a relationship with a *Playa*, the relationship is full of fake and shallow love. He is never satisfied with one girl because it is never enough to stroke his ego. Somewhere along his life, he lacked in love & affection, often from his parents, and needs to collect the hearts of women to feel important. So a *Playa* will do whatever it takes to get you to fall in love with him. Even if he has to lie about being in love and wanting to marry you. Hell, he might even marry you, but that won't stop him from falling in love and marrying someone else at the same damn time if he can get away with it.

That's why when you fall in love with a *Playa* your "relationship" is more like a *situationship* and it always "kind of *feels* like love" but the only person a *Playa* loves is himself. He doesn't really love you as a person; he loves the fact that YOU are in love with him. That's why you are usually left crushed at the end of this relationship because as soon as the excitement of you falling in love with him has died down, he is on to collect the next heart to add to his trophy collection.

Then you have the **Starters** who is actually playing the dating games to win games so he can get to the championship ring. He is in it for the love & relationships and to help you grow.

These men want something more profound than scoring points & collecting trophies. They're actually trying to win the game and make it to the championships to get the ring. These type of men are dating to find love and marriage. They want marriage because it adds to their overall life accomplishments and experience. And most importantly helps them get to the next level in life so they can grow as a person. The problem is they start something but never finish. The starters are more cautious with their moves and may move slower & take less risk. All of their moves are calculated which could come off a little less exciting compared to the *Playas*. A *Starter* may even confuse you into thinking they aren't interested. But it's not that they aren't interested they just are less enthused and more cautious about which relationships to get into and like to take things slow. They like to pull the "let's be friends first" card a lot. And there is nothing wrong with that. I actually prefer it that way, so my emotions don't get caught up too fast. But I don't want it to take FOREVER either, especially if I entered the dating game to find love not more "friends" to add to my contact lists. But if you don't understand how a *Starter* is playing his game and if not down with how he moves, he won't be afraid to give you the boot. They have no time for unnecessary hassle. And can keep you in the friend zone while he is out exploring if you let him.

Let's go back for a second. You see the *Playas are* more of the showoffs. They live their life on the edge and take more risks to keep the thrill of the game going. That's the reason they can win so many trophies because they are good at doing tricks if you catch my drift. Usually, they're personified as the bad boys, whereas the *Starters* are thinking more about the long run; they only want to win the games that will get them closer to that ring. They avoid spontaneity because they are not trying to jeopardize winning by getting hurt doing something dumb. They hardly truly get invested into anyone or "game" for this matter, unless they are sure it will benefit their life goals. They stick to the schedule and stick to the book of what they have to do. They play by the rules, and they just aren't as fired up when a new girl comes along, and that's no fun. That's why so many women complain that their relationship with men like this lack "passion," excitement and romance or if they are not in a confirmed relationships often have to ask these men "what are we?" The *Starters* are just slow at making moves and decisions and don't see the rush in making one. Like I said before, they start things but don't finish, especially, if you don't know how to get them to make a move without forcing it.

Most *Starters* like to operate in the gray-space of a relationship to leave room for genuine growth and maturation. They need to see how you can help them win at life. Although they can come off insensitive because they rarely lie about being in love or wanting marriage if that's not what they want with you, you will never find yourself emotional drained and heartbroken. The most you might find yourself getting is impatient with their indecision or maybe even bored to death.

I know what you are thinking, when does the game end for married men?

Because it feels like even married men are still playing games. And you know what? You're right. Some married men are still playing games because the game doesn't end once you are married that's when the games have just begun. The difference is married men are playing a whole different ball game that I won't even get into because I was never married before. But common sense tells me that the fundamentals of the game are still the same. Keep it fun, keep it challenging, overcome your hardships & battles with grace and always set new goals to strive for greatness. That's what makes a champ. If a man feels like his marriage is lacking in any of those areas better believe he will start scouting for new teammates and may even switch teams if he feels it beneficial to him and his goals in the long run. And vice versa. That's just how human beings operate. It's hard wired in their DNA.

Once we wake up to the harsh reality that people, even married people are only human and follow human nature of self-preservation first, then we will learn how to operate accordingly. I always told myself that if I ever got married, I would always stay prepared for the worst but strive for the best. The way I see it nothing last forever, not even this precious life in this body. But that doesn't mean you get lazy. You keep a positive mindset, always find new ways to grow and never be afraid to walk away if things aren't for your best interest. Life will go on, and these human social constructs that we try to uphold to unrealistic high regards can be the very thing that is causing all the pain and suffering when it comes to living life. If we learn how to let go and go with the flow, I believe life can be so easy. But this is a whole different topic for maybe a book in the future? My views on life and the social human construct as we know it.

But I will say this if I were playing the marriage game I would always incorporate these three strategies to help keep the marriage alive and well.

1. A Family Legacy Building Plan:

Once a champ of any game gets a ring they are now playing to leave their legacy behind & it is so very crucial to find a teammate who can help cater to that growth and ambition. If the couple cannot get on the same page as far as winning more games for the long-term, then the champ will start to look elsewhere for that support. Ask yourself do you help each other with your personal dreams, goals &

ambitions? Communication and the willingness to get on board and work together to make it happen are key elements if you want to implement this winning strategy.

2. A Fun, Excitement & Adventure Plan: (Keep the Bond Alive)

I don't care what anyone says no intends to be around someone who is boring all the time. If the excitement and thrill of the game are lost, then the marriage will get dull and boring. Just because you guys are working towards a long-term goal doesn't mean fun celebration or new challenging adventures can't be incorporated every once and awhile. Forget every once and a while it needs to be a part of your daily, weekly, monthly & yearly routine. Make the most out of life every day. For instance, celebrating small wins can give the marriage hope for the future. Doing creative projects like vlogging, doing little pranks & experiments with each other keeps the bond, joy, and laughter going. Also, different types of adventures would be, keeping the romance and sex hot and juicy, starting a new business and building wealth together, traveling to new places with each other, getting healthy and starting a spiritual journey together and so much more. Signs if your marriage is headed to a dreadful dullness is if you have too many days in a row where the routine is the same. Go to work, come home & watch tv, barely speaking, never building on new ideas, regular ass sex and the list goes on how to drain the life out of a marriage. The only time you feel your heart race is when y'all are having an argument, and that's never alright.

3. Emotional, Mental & Spiritual Wellness Plan.

How will you emotionally support each other when things get rough? How will you guys practice your spirituality, overcoming hardships and not letting defeat get the best of you? What kind of plans do you have to promote mental, emotional and physical health?

In life, there will be a lot of ups and downs good and bad, now multiple that by two since you will have a life partner to endure it with. So you have to have a plan in place. Back to my motto prepare for the worsts and strive for the best. Challenges promote growth and hardships can be a learning experience. But, too many difficulties and losses can drain you, so learning how to avoid altogether is a must. Not doing things that will jeopardize the marriage, like toxic behaviors such as infidelity, substance abuse, domestic violence- verbal and physical and so on then those things that can literally drain the life out of that marriage so having an agreement that those things won't be tolerated is a requirement.

I feel like if you can master these three strategies, then you can enjoy the game & keep playing for as long as it will last, or till death do you part, whichever comes first. But I must say this; I know in my heart of hearts that if you do everything with a good heart and EXPECT NOTHING in return, you will never be disappointed. The magic to happiness is to let go of expectations. Now, this doesn't mean let go of standards. Because if you don't stand for something your will fall for anything, more on that in another chapter. But you should let go of expectations. Meaning, let go of your strong beliefs on how you "think" things should go and how you think people "should" be, and just accept things, and people for who they truly are, then you will win every time. Because it's not about change; it's about acceptance, experience and growth.

by. Nancy Beauplan

"SOMETIMES IN EXCHANGE OF LEARNING THE GAME YOU HAVE TO GET PLAYED

3

Girl He's Playing You

Sometimes in exchange of learning the game
you have to get played

Unknown

So if you haven't realized it yet all men are players and everyone is being played. But let's be clear if still hasn't clicked just because all men are players doesn't mean they are all playing with the same intention. Some have good intentions, and some have not so good intentions, it's up to how you perceive it. You have to figure out what you will accept and what you will not. And it all starts with knowing what you want. What works for some might not work for all. It's not about what's right or wrong, good or bad; it's all about what you will accept and what makes you happy because a man is going to do what a man is going to do. But that doesn't mean you have to deal with it. You have the choice to walk away. Stick to your guns and make him rise to your standards. Become aware of the games he is playing and act accordingly. Don't be fooled by his words pay attention to his actions.

Now if you are reading this book without reading vol 1. Then you missed a very crucial chapter in the book called "Girl He's Playing You" So that's why I created this book as a separate guide book that reveal the big red flags and the scenarios of behaviors to look out for. Because I know you are wondering "how am I suppose to identify these men?" And

I'm even going to take it a step further and categorize each red flag with the different groups of men so you can know who you are dealing with as well.

It can be kind of hard to tell the difference because all of these men usually start the game the same, but end it entirely differently. Here is how I approach every situation. First I peep the situation if I feel some "type of way" about something I never sweep it under the rug anymore. I play close attention to what I am feeling. And then I address the incident to gain understanding. It's important to gain clarity from your partner because it is very easy to overreact to certain situations, especially in this day and age. But after my attempt to gain understanding and it still isn't clear then I say just trust your gut instinct. If you can't get it to be clear no matter how many dots he presents, if the dots can't connect, then you have to trust your woman's intuition. You may never get the truth, and you may never get to the bottom of it, and hey you may even lose out on a great person. But it is better to be safe than to be sorry. Most of the time your gut instinct is right. Love yourself enough first to know if you can't get clear on a situation it's always better to walk away.

So here are the red flags you must never ignore.

4

The Benchwarmers

Let's start with the benchwarmers. Benchwarmers are real dickheads cause all they think is with their dick-head. They are very disrespectful to women very objectifying & all they talk about is sex, your body and your appearance and could care less about the girl, her feelings or your values. Their primary goal is to use your body as an object to please & relieve themselves. If you identified one of these men as a benchwarmer, please run far away as soon as possible.

Now if you are just looking for sex as well then hook up with a benchwarmer, and it's all good. No one feelings get hurt, and no emotions get involved.

But if you are looking for a life partner, You can't turn a hoe into a husband; there is no hope when dealing with a man at this stage. It's levels to this dating game, and if you are looking for a husband, you aren't going to get it at level one.

HEY BABY YOU SO FINE, YOU SO FINE, YOU BLOW MY MIND

The Situation

You go on a date, and it seems that he can never look you in your eyes. Every time you look up at him, he either has his eyes on your breast, your hips or your butt. And before you can even get dinner started the conversation quickly gets into your sex life and what you can do in the bedroom. And then when you try to redirect the convo he pressures you to loosen up and even tries to insult your intelligence by calling you a "goody two-shoes" or uptight.

<u>Your wishful thinking:</u>

I'm an adult; we are all grown here. I can handle a little adult conversation. I don't want him to think I am too uptight and can't have a little fun. I don't want him to lose interest in me. That's true if that's what you came for and an adult who can handle it. But if you did not then you need to shut it down immediately.

The reality:

My guy friend always used to tell me "if a guy wants to see if you are a hoe, he is going to test the waters and treat you like one." He knows what he is doing by asking you inappropriate questions. Especially when you first meet. But I realized the guys who aren't so pressed about sex never really ask. They don't act like horny little teenagers who never got any before. People who never have any sex only want to talk about is sex.

The solution:

If you were looking for sex, then engage in this type of sexivity. But if you are looking for love and a real relationship, in the long run, address the situation head on and tell him you are not comfortable talking about your sex life and you can even flip the switch on him and make him feel insecure by asking,

"you never had sex before?
why are you acting like a horny little boy?"

And if he still won't cut it out, then cut the date short. Always have you an emergency exit strategy and never deal with him again. There is no need to endure an uncomfortable date that is not going anywhere. It's your life; you are in control.

by. Nancy Beauplan

"HIT IT AND QUIT IT."

The situation:

Ok, so you ignored the 1st sign completely cause he was really good at sweet talking you and making you feel comfortable. So you gave up the goods. He seemed like a pretty nice guy and you was like screw it you only live once. After its all said and done, (sex) he decided he can't spend the night. Or even worst you can't spend the night. Cool. Right? Wrong! Because then he says he will call you and you never hear from him ever again. You make attempts to reach out, but he ignores you as if you two never existed.

Your wishful thinking:

I know we had a connection, maybe something happened to him. I hope he is ok. You start blaming yourself, thinking you did something wrong and you weren't great in bed. Then you may even go into a phase of "I knew what I was getting myself into." But the denial of the possibility that you may have gotten played keeps haunting you. So you call, and you call, and you call, and nothing.

The reality:

He just hit it & quit it. You are not going to hear from him cause he got what he wanted out of you and now he is on to the next. He is ignoring your calls because you let him hit on the first attempt. That's his game and no matter how grown up you are about it, the honor and possibility of being in a relationship are lost because in his mind he has already won.

The solution:

The only thing you can do is to charge it to the game. Don't blow his phone up, don't try to embarrass him, just charge it and learn from your mistake. I always advise wait at least three months to find out if this is the guy you don't mind getting played by before you have sex, because that is what you are up against and never let him hit on the first night even if you are ready for the repercussions.

HEY STRANGER, HEY BIG HEAD, HEY "OTHER PET NAME" THAT I HAVE NO BUSINESS CALLING YOU.

The situation:

So he "hit it and quit it," you charged it to the game and finally managed to forget about him. Now you are finally getting it together and moving on with your life. Then all of a sudden he hit your phone with the "hey stranger" text out of nowhere. Maybe you posted a picture on Instagram, and he saw you glow up, and now he's in your inbox trying to see what's up.

<u>Your wishful thinking:</u>

I knew I been on his mind, about time he hits me up. We are meant to be with each other. A passionate love like that could never be forgotten. I'm Interested to see where he has been. It must be a real good explanation why he would just disappear like that.

The reality:

He is bored, horny and needs someone to pass the time with until his "hey stranger" text comes through from the real love of his life, cause you know she is probably busy somewhere ignoring him too.

If you hook up with him again, he will go ghost on you again guarantee it. And that's the number 1 way to form a "friends with benefits" type of situation. If a man is into you, he is into you he is not going to go ghost on you with no real explanation. He won't go ghost for weeks with no contact. He will answer when you call and make conversation about things that interest you, not just sex.

He is just trying to see if he still got it. He wants to know that he still has that control over you. Men like this love to compete with other men for women to prove their masculinity. So to feel like that alpha male again, he's going to pull that card. He is going to front to his friends like "I already had her and I could get her again." So now you've become like a little toy to him a little game that he wants to play for his satisfaction to boost his ego even more. So don't fall into that trap here is what you do.

The solution:

Call him out on his BS play him like he played you and tell him you're not interested. Tell him you're not a toy that he can pick up when he is bored. You've been calling him he hasn't been responding so he can lose your number like he has been doing. Or even better just ignore him altogether like he doesn't exist just like he treated you. And watch him drive himself crazy trying to chase you for a period until he gets impatient. But never be so desperate to answer his first attempt to reach out to you when you've reached out to him several times and got no response. Show him that you are strong and won't tolerate his mess.

5

<u>The Playas</u>

If you are reading this book then more than likely you are dealing with a Playa. And if you read my last book, I broke down a whole list of scenarios to identify a "Playa." and all of their lying, sneaky, manipulative ways if you found yourself in a relationship with them. But how do you spot one if you have never dealt with one before?

by. Nancy Beauplan

I JUST MET YOU BUT I KNOW YOU ARE THE ONE!

The Situation:

As soon as you meet a Playa, he's already head over heels in love with you. Within the first week, he is already professing his love to you and telling you how much he can't live without you. He tells you, "you are his wife" and continues to feed you a whole bunch of sweet nothings and makes big promises to you. He puts you on a pedestal somewhere in fantasy land, and this date is like a Fairytale from Heaven. The relationship is moving super duper fast like a tornado. Magically you seem to have everything in common, and he finds everything you do interesting. You are so caught up you start to believe all the lies he is telling you. You become blinded from what's real and what's not.

Your wishful thinking:

I have finally found the one. Just like the movies, this man treats me like a queen and I didn't even have to wait all that time to find him. This relationship is full of passion and I didn't have to settle cause he knows what he wants

The reality:

Playas fall in love like they pick draws. It's just that easy for them. Getting someone to fall in love with them is their mission because they don't know how to love themselves. When you meet a man, who is all in love with you so easily, always ask yourself one question, How?? This man just met you, and he knows you well enough to want you to be his wife?

The solution:

Question everything, especially if it's creeping you out that he can fall in love with you so easily. Ask him "how is he so in love with you?" Then pay close attention to the life he lives, does he even love himself, what is his past relationships with other women. What is his relationship with his mother? Don't follow him into this whirlwind love affair until you are ready not because he is pressuring you to feel the love. Be careful cause the faster you fall in love, the harder you hit the ground.

ALL WOMEN ARE EVIL EXCEPT FOR YOU OF COURSE.

The Situation:

Every woman he has ever dated has done him wrong and cheated. He just is looking for the one but can't catch a break. He talks horribly about his ex or baby mama to make them seem like the enemy.

<u>Your wishful thinking:</u>

Well he is probably tired of getting hurt and really wants to make this work with me. So I am going to give him my all so he never has to feel that pain again. I am going to prove to him that I am different and he can put his faith in me.

<u>The reality:</u>

You are what you attract. So if every woman before him has done him wrong and hurt him, can you imagine what kind of person he had to be to make to attract that? If he can't say one nice thing about a woman, he has dealt with prior to you and is always the victim you can already tell he is playing you.

HE SAYS "YOU ARE TOO GOOD FOR HIM"

The situation:

He goes on these long rants about you deserving better and how he doesn't deserve you. He goes on and says he is afraid to disappoint you and can't believe you are still sticking by his side. He is basically throwing a pity party about how awful he is and how awesome you are. And even questions your motives for being with him. He can't understand why you would want to be with him when there are "so many other good men out there" who are better than him educationally, financially and emotionally. He vows to "TRY" to do better. But of course, he can only try.

<u>Your wishful thinking:</u>

My man appreciates me and is just being modest. I am so lucky to have a man who knows what he has and he will never loose that for a quick shot of pussy. I'm going to stick it out with him and prove to him I love him just the way he is. I'm not a gold digger like these other females. He truly does make me happy, and that's all that matters.

by. Nancy Beauplan

Harsh Reality:

When a man tells you that you deserve better, believe him and RUN! He is being dead honest with you. In the beginning he just swore up and down you were the one and now the story has changed. He knows what kind of dog he is. The guilt is literally eating him up inside, and he just wishes you dumped him already. He is trying to push you away gently so he can enjoy his dog ways. Men are very prideful egotistical beings. The mere thought of being compared to the next man will have him libbed. So to have him blatantly downplay himself to you should be a clear-cut red flag that, Girl, he is playing you!!

He accuses you of "Messing Around"

by. Nancy Beauplan

The situation:

Every little thing you do, he makes a big deal about it and accentuates that you are cheating. For instance, he goes through your phone out of nowhere picks out the most basic text to a male pal of yours and excuses you of cheating with him. In your mind you know he is trippin' because you don't even find the guy attractive but he blows it up way out of proportion. It even has you thinking, "have I been a little too friendly with my buddy ole' pal?" Suddenly the arguments come out of nowhere, usually triggered by him. And he has these long-winded rants about nothing. Then starts picking on you for any little thing you may do. Like on the very rare occasion you miss his call.

Your wishful thinking:

My baby is just a little jealous. Maybe I have been a little bit too friendly with my homeboi. I need to cut off my male friends, so he doesn't think I am doing anything with them. You may even believe that it's a natural behavior for "dominate" men to act out this way and might even find it a little attractive. You feel like he is just trying to protect what's his and would be devastated if you ran off with someone else.

by. Nancy Beauplan

Harsh Reality:

He is so guilty and so nervous of getting caught, everything you do reminds him of what he is doing, and in actuality, he is just trying to get some dirt on you just in case you find out that, girl, he is playing you!

I'M IN A RELATIONSHIP BUT I NEED HELP GETTING OUT

The Situation:

He is married or in a relationship but claims he is miserable but still hasn't left. He claims he should have married you. He just needs to find a way to get out of it. He tells you things are going to get worked out just believe in him and keep being strong while he sorts out this madness.

<u>Your wishful thinking:</u>

This is something I have dealt with first hand. He is miserable and really loves me, but he just can't find the strength to leave. The right time will come, and soon he will be all mine. I just have to be patient.

The Reality:

The right time will never come because if he were that miserable, trust he would have found a way out. Under no circumstance is it ok to be what this generation call's "the side-chick" NO matter how he tries to flips it or explains it. If he is in a relationship, and you know about it, you are the side-chick. And it proves to you what kind of man he is if he would cheat on his wife with you. If he would do that to his wife, someone he made a sacred vow to in front of God, what makes you think he won't cheat on you as well? Or even worst lead you into a land of broken promises, lies & mistreatment. Where nothing happens, and nothing gets better. Girl! He is playing you!

The solution:

Never date a man while he is dating or married to another woman. It never works out the way you planned. But if you insist on doing this, which I recommend you don't, make sure everyone is in the know. NO secrets and out in the open. And once everything is exposed you will see where you stand from there.

6

The Starters

The starters are typically good men, but they are also so busy trying to build themselves up and get their lives in order, they don't even realize the emotional rollercoaster they are putting women through. That's why I still list them as a player in the game because even though their intention wasn't to play with you or manipulate you. Some things they do can leave you feeling confused, played and bitter about where you stand in a relationship with them. So I am just going to list situations that you may interpret as some red flags that will help you identify them as a Starter or not.

SHE'S JUST A FRIEND, YOU'RE JUST A FRIEND, WE ARE ALL JUST FRIENDS!

The Situation:

A starter may have a lot of female friends. They may even treat you like a friend but may have approached you as a potential mate and may have even crossed the boundaries like a lover. But you soon realize he is surrounded by friendly women who are available to him. It seems like he always keeps women around him and even invites them in your circle. There is no hiding it, and he may even introduce you to them as a friend. *How great a new friend in the circle.* You haven't gotten intimate yet so you know you can't trip, but you are taken aback by it. Because the way this man move is so damn direct.

Your Wishful Thinking

Wow, I have a lot of competition, and I have to really put myself out there to get his attention. Let me make it be known that I am really feeling him so he can choose me and leave these other dusty broads alone. And let me even ask him "what are we?" so he knows I am not playing this "friendly" game with him.

The Harsh reality:

The reality is you have a little competition. This commitment to a relationship is not going to come easy. But if you feel like this man is worth it and you guys can have a potential future together, don't get intimated by his female friends. Stand your ground, and continue to let him chase you. Don't get childish and demand him to cut off his female friends though. And don't require him to give you a title when you just met and starting to get to know each other. I know you are feeling anxious because you want a man. Girl I know. But you are going to chase his ass off like that. And when he cuts you off you will start to feel bitter and tempted to play the "all men ain't shit" card. You see this game you are playing with the Starter is all about patience. Don't get desperate and be at his every beckon call hoping to get his attention, because that will quickly land you in the friend zone for life.

The solution

Please take it slow. Follow his lead, but peak his interest. Give him the challenge he is looking for but be woman enough to know they are other women playing for the spot. This is the definition of real life dating. Just because he is spending money and spending time with you doesn't mean he isn't doing it with other women. And he is not going to hide the fact that he is either. If you haven't had the conversation that you guys are in a committed relationship, don't assume he knows. Even if you had sex with him don't assume he knows he is in a committed relationship with you.

That's why it's important to know the rules of the dating game. Sex is always welcomed but is never required and is never the determining factor if you are in a committed relationship or not. Having a grown communication about it is the only way to know with these men.

Now if you give him sex with him before you get a commitment then you are walking a very fine line because he may commit or he may not. But that's the dangerous game you play. So hold out on sex. Giving it up early will not put you ahead of his other female friends. Building a bond and getting on the same page will. But always keep that sexual spark going, so he knows there is something to look forward to if he does commit

by. Nancy Beauplan

"I'M BUSY, CAN I GET A RAIN CHECK?"

The situation:

He doesn't prioritize you at all. After the first date, he hasn't made an effort to plan another one. He only seems to hit you up when he needs to borrow something or needs help with something. He doesn't ignore your calls, but when you talk it's very short and boring.

Your wishful thinking:

This man is not feeling me. He must be busy with his other female friends. I knew he was full of shit. And every time we talk it is so dead and boring. This dude is not my type. I need some excitement and passion. I need to look for a guy that's fun like my ex but without the drama.

The reality:

You don't need to look for a man like your ex! You have a good man right in front of you, it's just that this man is busy building his life. If you are going to date cool, but if you can't help him with what he is working on you guys won't spend much time together. That's why it's important to find someone who is passionate about what you are passionate about. If you guys aren't interested in the same hobby, you aren't going to hang out much. Especially, if that means the only time y'all link up, it's about spending money on dinner and a date. *That man ain't got time for that.* If you don't learn how to get on the same page with him, you might miss out on a good man. So here is what you do.

The solution:

First, make sure he is really doing what he say's he is doing. That means make sure he is busy working on his side projects & hustles and not busy booed up with some girl. Then when you verify it's not another chick, substance abuse or laziness, because men do cheat on you with different things other than girls, learn how to get into what he is into. So if he is into fitness, find out how you guys can do some training together. If he is busy working on a new creative project like photography, find out how you can help. Honestly, that may be the only time you get to see him and spend time with him outside of the typical dating scene. If he wants to invite you into his hobbies and passions, don't be so boujee to the point you feel *"some type of way"* because it isn't a real date. I know you are wondering when is he going to wine and dine you, but that man is trying to save his money. So get in where you fit in. It will be fun, it will be relaxed, and it will be worth it in the long run.

by. Nancy Beauplan

YOU KNEW I WASN'T LOOKING FOR A RELATIONSHIP...

The situation:

So you guys been hanging out, even had sex a few times and you started getting deep feelings for him. You tried to get him to commit to a relationship, and he says "he just want's to be friends." But you decided to continue giving up the goods and completely ignore the fact that he said: "he did not want to be in a committed relationship." Then all of sudden you try to check him about something, and he hit you with the "hold up we're just friends... you knew I wasn't looking for a relationship." Now you mad and reading this book.

Your wishful thinking:

You know you should cut him off, but you stay in hopes that he will realize you are the one for him. You feel like you can convince him into being in a relationship with you. So maybe if you get a little extra clingy & continue to put the pussy on him, then he will finally come around. Or better yet, how about you get pregnant and have a baby and he will step up to the plate for sure, and you guys can be a big happy family... Sike!

The Harsh Reality:

He just brought you back down to the friend zone that you tried to escape from. And you might be there for life if you continue to think you can change his mind. The man clearly stated he didn't want a committed relationship with you. And like I said before, sex is always welcomed but is never required and is not the signifier of being in a committed relationship. This man enjoys his "freinds with benefits" relationship with you, and he will be damned if changes just because you asked. The crazy part about it is you may find out that a few months later, he ran off and married someone else even though he told you he didn't want to be in a committed relationship. That doesn't make him a dog that just makes him honest. And that's the risk you take when playing the game with a Starter.

The solution:

Don't be nice about this situation. You must leave the moment he says he isn't looking for a relationship. Don't try to change his mind or convince him of anything. Cut him off from sex and cut the convo short. He will either disappear from your life or realize he messed up big time and try to get you back. Either way, you will win because you won't be getting played.

In conclusion:

When it's all said and done it all boils down to "what kind of woman you are, and that will determine which type of Player you will attract. Because let's be honest no matter how great a guy is he has been every type of player in the book.

For instance, all men can be a Benchwarmer if he is dealing with a hoe. And all men can also be a Playa if he is dealing with a girl who is a doormat & refuses to stand up for herself. Furthermore, every man can be a Starter if he see's a woman who can add value to his life for the long run. That's why you can date a man who treated you like shit and then a few months later he is "so called" married to the love of his life. At the core, these men are, who they are, but it's up to you to accept them or not. You can't change them you can only show them your worth, and if he feels compelled to be with you, then he will find it within himself to do the work to rise to your standards.

That's why you have to have patience. Wait at least 90 days before you commit or jump into anything with anyone. And yes that even means sex! Three months is a good way to see someone's intentions because nature shows every three months a new season will happen. People's true colors will start to appear. And it's more than just about waiting; you have to pay attention to the red flags I mentioned earlier.

And most importantly, you have to let go of the notion of molding a man into what you want him to be. There is a difference between molding him and making him step up to the plate. Every man has to choose to step up to the plate. It all boils down to what kind of woman are you and what you are are attracting. So the real question is, what kind of woman are you?

"IF YOU PUT UP WITH IT, YOU ARE GOING TO END UP WITH IT. SET THE STANDARD YOU WANT AND DON'T SETTLE FOR LESS."

7

NICE GIRLS FINISH SAD, MAD & LONELY

"If you put up with it, you are going to end up with it. Set the standard you want and don't settle for less."

Dr. Steve Maraboli

Are you too nice for your own good? I know we'd all like to think of ourselves as nice. But is your nice the healthy version, or the anxious to please version? How do you tell the difference? Well if you find yourself being a slave to the nice label, and think that just because you are nice to people, then you are worthy of their love, that's the first sign of knowing you are upholding an unhealthy version of nice.

You have to learn how to find a healthy balance between being nice and being assertive and standing your ground, especially when you are in relationships. If you don't learn how to stand up for yourself, then you will find yourself being walked all over, taken for granted and ultimately unhappy and lonely at the end because people don't want to be around anyone who is unhappy.

I know all the pains of being the too nice girl. And I feel like that was the main reason why I was so prone to get hurt & my heart broken.

So here is how I learned how to stop

being so damn nice and actually start standing up for myself and demanding what I want out of any relationship.

1. I stopped being nice to people when I felt like they were ignoring me or I was being insulted. I learned to give people the energy they gave me. So if I was dating a guy and he stopped answering my calls and my texts and started being distant. I never protested and took the blame for it. I reciprocated his same actions to him, and once he got a taste of his own medicine, he either would retreat or advance. Either way, I won because I was not giving more than required of me, so I never felt like I was being robbed, used or taken for granted.

2. I stopped being overly concerned about whether people liked me or not and

I stopped kissing people's ass. I learned that the people who are meant to be in my life would match my vibe. And if our vibes don't match then it wasn't meant for me.

3. I stopped over-apologizing for stuff. If there wasn't a true offense occurring then what the hell was I apologizing for? I learned to save my sorry's for when they were needed and just because someone had a different point of view, felt some type of way or had an objection about something didn't mean it required a sorry especially if I didn't do anything wrong to hurt them.

4. I learned that just because you are my family, lover or friend doesn't mean you are any less human. If I wouldn't let a stranger get away with doing something wrong to me, then I shouldn't minimize

your faults either. So I learned how to address things that didn't make me happy, comfortable or hurt me in any type of way. I learned that if I didn't speak up and say something soon enough, then I would be the only one carrying the burden of the pain for a lifetime, while you were sleeping well at night unbothered and that just isn't fair. That type of imbalance in a relationship will cause a resentment, and eventually over time will ruin what I was trying to save in the first place by not saying something sooner.

5. I learned that it was ok to feel legitimate anger without being horrified or ashamed of myself when I did get upset with my partner or friend. Instead of feeling like I have ruined everything, I kept in mind that what is meant for me will be for me and what isn't will be on its merry

way. I can not hold on to anything that doesn't want to stay because they can't handle my reaction to something they did wrong.

6. And last but not least, You have to make people earn a spot in your life. Don't just give away all of your love, emotions and everything you have to them for free. And when I say free I am not talking about money. I am talking about reciprocation. Did they exchange love & emotions for yours or did you just give it in "hopes" they would give it back? That's why after you got your heartbroken you feel empty and may feel like that person has something of yours that you want back.

You learned to depend on this person for love and completeness. So when the relationship is over, it feels like you are now half of a person and all you want is your wholeness back and it makes it super hard for you to walk away. So that's why it's important to be whole before you go and join forces with someone. You need to learn how to fill your cup up firsts and give whatever extra that is flowing over.

Also, it is crucial to make sure you are always getting something out of any relationship you decide to invest time, energy and love into, don't just bank on the hope that someday you will get it back. But always be in the position that if you had to leave that person on any given day, you can say "I really enjoyed that experience, we shared so much together, but I can leave with my dignity in knowing I didn't give more than what was given to me. Instead of crying that "we made so many plans, I gave him so much of me and got nothing back." You should never feel empty after a relationship is over. You should feel experienced that's the goal.

An equal exchange of something that you are willing to give in order to gain. And it's all different and unique for everyone. But you have to get clear about what is you want before you go investing into someone and make sure they do what they have to do to it earn it. That is the only way someone is going to cherish what they earned. If they worked hard for a spot in your life on a consistent basis, do you think they will jeopardize all of their investments into you, emotionally, physically spiritually and mentally?

No, they would think twice about doing something to hurt you or jeopardize that. But if you gave it all away so freely in the beginning because you were "too nice" then you will lose at the end because that person will just take from you and give nothing in return. And when he gives nothing, it will be so easy to walk away and throw out what you gave because it was free he didn't take a loss.

It is all about setting your standards high and learning how to put men in their place or walk away when they try to bring you down or misuse you. This phase may be an ugly stage for you because I know as the "nice girl" it is kind of hard to stand up for yourself. The process may be a bit ugly, but it is so worth it at the end. You have to stick to your guns. And it all starts with knowing what do you want.

It's important to know before entering a relationship, and keeping these six things in mind, will help you figure out what you want out the relationship.

And since the topic is love before getting into any Loveship, the best way to find out what you want is to determine your love language.

According to Chapman, there are five ways to express and experience love, here they are:

1. Gift Giving,
2. quality time,
3. words of affirmation & appreciation
4. acts of service (devotion),
5. and physical touch.

It's important to know which of these matter to you the most because when entering the dating game and choosing someone to invest your emotions, time & energy into you have to be sure you that person can give you what you need.

So what's the definition of love for you? what does it look like and feel like? And have you mastered giving it to yourself before you go out looking for it somewhere else? And yes that even means physical touch. No matter what you create your wholeness. And under no circumstance should it be dependent on other people.

Then have you established deal breakers? What makes achieving it worth it and what makes it not. These are all of the things that are important to know before letting people into your world.

So say if you meet a guy, and you're like Nancy I see this guy, and I believe in his potential do you help him or still focus on yourself? I know a lot of women do this especially if they feel their man will be well paid in the future, like an athlete or celebrity. Then you first need to have that conversation with him; you can't just be secretly trying to help him and expecting something in the future for it, that's how you create resentment.

Once you have that conversation with him and you guys are on the same page as far as, being partners in this come up is concerned, then you have to always keep in mind these three rules.

These are three things you should never endure no matter how nice you are.

1. being dependent

2. putting your dreams on hold and if you do decide to put all your focus on his goals then

3. never, ever live in the shadows while doing it.

Here is why:

I see a lot of instances where women work really hard on bringing a guy to the top and get left by the wayside cause they stopped working on themselves and exclusively helped him. That's why it's important to have your own passion & your own vision. Stay glowed up and keep growing. Never stop growing cause you are trying to help someone else.

Also, I understand a man has to be a man but what does that have to do with you being a dependent on him? You mean to tell me a man can't be a man unless he has a woman to depend on him. Especially if you aren't married? And even if you are married, you guys should definitely work together in a partnership to build any empire.

Never be at the mercy of someone when

you are in a relationship. You should have your own, and he should have his own and then when guys come together you can build up on top of that. Never let him count you out. You can be supportive to your man but always be able to bring something to the table and make sure you get credit for it. Never do the work in the shadows. Even the president of the United States has to acknowledge his wife as the first lady, and she has to bring some initiatives to work on while they are in the white house.

And if you have a dream always go after your dreams wholeheartedly because if you don't for the sake of the relationship then trust and believe there is a chance he will leave you for someone who did. Like I said before, frequencies have to match. A boss is going to find someone who bossed up their life to match their hustle. I see so many basketball wives or celebrity wives who held it down in silence in the shadows for their husbands, and the only time you hear about them is when they are about to get a divorce. What sense does that make? You mean to tell me you been home raising his kids, putting your dreams on hold and now you want a divorce to be with some chick you met while you were on the road? You got me all the way fucked up.

If the dream is to be on the road and you want me to be your wife and have a family, then that means this plan needs to built as a family trip because you did not sign up to be a house sitter. That's why it's super important to be on the same page with your man. If not it can really put you in a bad position. Don't be entirely dependent on him with no say so in what is going on. Because when it all blows up, you will be the one looking crazy in the media as the greedy, bitter, ex-wife who just wants spousal support and child support.

"IF YOU ARE LOSING AT A GAME, CHANGE THE GAME.

8

How to change the game

If you are losing at a game, change the game.
Gregory Benford

So far, this whole book has been about how men are playing the game and who you have to be to fit in it. And I started it like that because that's how most women think. And that is the main reason why they are losing. They are too worried about who they have to be for a man. But if you want to change the game you have to create your own rules. You have to stop worrying about what a man wants and what kind of game he is playing and start asking yourself "what the hell do I want?"

What makes the game worth while playing for me? What kind of game do I want to play? See when you create your own game and start figuring out what you want then you become a bit more of a challenge for these men. And all men love a good challenge. One they have never conquered before. One that is unique and no one has ever played except for them.

There was a time I used to hear the phrase "Hoes is winning, " and I used to wonder how and why? Then finally I figured it out. It wasn't really because they were highly sexual or half naked on the screen; that might have a little bit to do it with it, but it wasn't the only reason it was something deeper. The main reason was because of the thrill of the whole thing. These women changed the game and started playing for them. They added a challenge to a game that they used to be once shamed out of playing. They started owning their shit by being true to who they are. They knew what they wanted out of a man before a man even approached them. And as a result, you had a bunch of men who have never seen this boldness in the sport before. It was a new challenge to either try to save her, conquer her or defeat her.

These women have created their own world with their own rules & they have a bunch of men who are dying to get a taste and figure it all out.

So what can we learn from our more liberated sisters? It's all about doing you. They created the rules and demanded what they want out of it and now they have men chasing them trying to convince them to switch and play their old game.

Now by no means, I am not telling you to start behaving in ways that are not in your character. Because it's not about what you do, it is the attitude you have while doing it. Please stay true to your conservative lifestyle. But never be afraid to ask for what you want. Stop giving, giving & giving ahead of time hoping and praying these men will figure out what you want. How about you tell them exactly what you need so there can be some type of equal reciprocation occurring, that way you won't feel like you are getting the short end of the stick.

The days of being a nice, passive,

unexpressive, people-pleasing woman are over. No more hidden agendas; don't get into a relationship unless he proves he can give you what you need. There are a billion people on the planet. NO need to fall for the first guy who has fallen into your honey trap.

And speaking of the honey trap, once you create your game and figure out what you want and who you want to play you have to set a honey trap. You have to find a way to make sure the right type of men is being attracted to you. In this day and age of technology and social media, there is no reason to work with just whatever just comes buzzing.

There is such a thing as having standards and not settling for less.

So how do you get these men to be

attracted to you? I live by the motto. Be the Honey which means to be so dope they can't ignore you. How do you be the honey, of course, you are probably thinking its all about looks. And while that is important it is not what gets the men to stick.

You have to figure out how you can get these men to learn about your abilities to help them. What kind of problems or desires can you help these men solve or achieve? And how will you get them to know about it? And thanks to social media you can set up all types of honey traps. And it doesn't mean you have to take off your clothes. It just means you have to be the best version of yourself inside and out. And share who you are with the world. By sharing and being transparent, you give them a sneak peak of who you are and what you bring to the table. That doesn't mean give it all up and bust it wide open for the gram. But just share your values, your insights and yes your beautiful ass selfies. Be true to what you enjoy don't fake the funk. And the people who are interested will do the work to get on a deeper level with you. And that's when you start making some real connections.

And once you made a connection it doesn't stop there, that is just the initial attraction. To build a bond and relationship with someone you have to tap into something of their interest other than sex, love, and marriage. Most women think that when you meet a guy, the convo should automatically talk about full blown commit, ties, marriage and family.

I want you to think back when you were younger and you fell in love with someone genuinely not because society told you that's what boys and girls had to to do. You fell in love because you and this boy had many interactions with each other and realized you had a common interest. The love didn't come first; maybe a slight attraction but it was always the common interest that took it to the next level of falling in love.

So the same rules apply when you meet a man now. After the initial attraction to each other, You have to find something you both are interested in, and then you have to find a way work together and excelling in that interest. That's how a relationship can genuinely work overtime. For instance, if you both are into health and fitness how can you guys work together to excel at it? What about building wealth, find ways you two can work together to be wealthy and feed off of each other's enthusiasm. What about spirituality, traveling, creativity, expanding your knowledge. There are so many ways to connect to someone without it always being about looks, sex, love & marriage that's only one part. Those are the results after what comes first. Finding a common interest and then working together passionately to excel, succeed or prevail in that common interest.

So say if you are like Nancy I'm not interested in anything I just want be a housewife like the old days, build a family support, my husband. Well, that's where you may fail sis. Cause if you are not interested in anything outside of that then you become uninteresting and that relationship will be boring and die. And having a child with someone can only keep someone's attention for so long. So this is where your personal self-work has to come in. You have to get interested in something. A craft, a hobby, a business of some type. When you do your self-development work, you find what is interesting to you.

You have to find something to throw yourself wholeheartedly. And here is the kicker it has to be true to you. Don't get interested in something because you want to get that man to notice you. That is not how it works. It has to be something all your own. That's why couples like a Jay-z and Beyonce can work. Cause they are both interested in music, outside of each other. That's what they did before they met. And then they decided to dominate the music industry together once they got into a relationship.

It's important to be intensely interested into something with or without him because that's when you will genuinely learn advanced tricks that can help anyone take their craft to the next level. And vice versa. For instance, if you love photography and you learned every corner of if just from the pure love then when you meet a man who is interested in that you can teach him some things. That's when you become attractive and valuable to a person, and that's what makes someone want to keep you around.

If you find that you guys are interested in something, then you can share your goals and see if he would be interested in helping you achieve them. It's all about getting in where you guys can click. If a person can't help you or there is no room in your life for them to participate how do you expect to keep the bond alive. And even if it is just to help raise the kids & pay the bills how will you make it interesting?

Whether you like to believe it or not those things get boring over time and any sane human being will soon get uninterested and detach.

So you are probably saying what if I am super boring and all I like to do is go out to eat. Well, why don't you set a goal for it? Here is how you set a goal, "I want to visit a new restaurant in 12 different cities in the next six months." You see how things can get interesting there. Keep it fun, keep it interesting. You can't keep living these boring existences and expect people to want to tag along with you for the heck of it.

To change the game, you always have

to have goals you are striving for in every area in your life. They reason why is because one, it is a productive thing to do if you want to have an ultimate life experience. And two because when you meet someone and expressing your interest, you guys can form a deeper bond around that interest.

So putting effort into these areas in your life is a good starting point to being attractive.

1. Appearance: do you put effort into your, fitness, hygiene and fashions?

2. Personality: does your spirit shine through?

3. Expression: do you say what you mean and mean what you say?

4. transparency: are you open and comfortable with your elf?

5. value contribution to the world: in what ways are you overall helping the

planet.

6. honesty in action: are you honest with people even when it doesn't feel good?

7. Evolution: how are you growing every day?

8. Having fun: do you just let go and be free from time to time?

You don't have to be this complete package to attract Mr. Right you have to be at least trying, though. Have a plan in place to achieve these goals.

Which brings me to my next point you have to put in the effort. There are a billion people on the planet. Just like you are not willing to settle for anyone, no one is going to settle for you. And you shouldn't want them to. I know you want people to accept you for who you are, just as you are, but that doesn't mean you can be lazy and not put any effort into self-development. You always want the right type of people around you. And all that means is the energetic frequencies have to match. So put out what you want to get back.

JUST A FEW LAST THINGS TO KEEP IN MIND ON THIS JOURNEY...

by. Nancy Beauplan

"YOU CAN'T RUSH SOMETHING YOU WANT TO LAST FOREVER

9

Patience

You can't rush something you want to last forever
Unknown

No matter what you do, remember always to have patience. Because at the end of the day that's the only thing that wins this game. You can't rush any process, from falling in love to healing from a heartbreak there is no quick fix.

So enjoy every aspect of the dating game. From every rejection to every rejoice, it is all an experience to appreciate. For instance, if you find out you are dealing with a Benchwarmer enjoy the turn-up while it last. Don't go trying to change that person. Learn what you don't like, call it for what it is, get the experience you can get out of it and move on to the next until you find what you are looking for. If you end up with a Playa, enjoy the thrill of falling in love and enduring the tough times that come with dealing with a Playa. And if you end up with a Starter enjoy all of the new outing experiences and bonding you will do. And when it is time to let go and move on don't hold onto anything or anyone that is not meant to grow with you.

It's ok to enjoy the game just as much as the fellas do. Always keep the big picture in the back of your head, but you don't have to stress about it everyday. Just try to stay in the present moment of the experience and always remember what you want. If you want fun, then make sure you are doing things in the relationship to ensure that fun exists. Like dates, trips, shopping, meals, quality time, bomb ass sex, family engagement, get what you need out of the relationship while being present. Worry about the day to day interactions, and when you feel in your heart to take it to the next level, for instance, emotional support and love then make sure that person you are dating is on the same page. Don't try to get emotional support out of someone who isn't emotionally available. Remember for each level there is a different devil to deal with, so don't rush something that isn't ready.

NOTHING LASTS FOREVER, SO LIVE IT UP, DRINK IT DOWN, LAUGH IT OFF, AVOID THE BULLSHIT, TAKE CHANCES NEVER HAVE REGRETS BECAUSE AT ONE POINT EVERYTHING YOU DID WAS EXACTLY WHAT YOU WANTED.

-MARYLIN MONROE

10

Get in The Game

If you want something go get it. Period!
Pursuit of Happiness

You can't be afraid to get in the game. Finding the right man to be in love with is so beautiful if you let it, but you can't be afraid to be open yourself up to it. Don't let the heartbreak of past relationships cripple you. Get in the game and enjoy the process. You can't just sit in your room hoping it finds you there.

So start by taking yourself out on dates. Learn what you like about the world. Get dressed and love on yourself first and set the tone for what you want.

If you want to get over your ex, you have to move on to the next.

And the more men you have on your radar, the less stressful it will be to find love. So make connections, form friendships and build relationships.

I come to the realization that the person you was so in love with had less to do with how great of a person he was, and more to do with filling a void of connection. Honestly, you might just need a male friend to exchange energy with.

Don't underestimate the power of connection. Some of you don't need to be in relationships some of you just need some male friends to exchange some masculine energy with. And if it turns into love and infatuation that's even more perfect. There are plenty of people out in the world who can give you that. But you have to go out and meet them.

Knowing all this information is worthless if you don't go out and do it. Go where the men are. Or more importantly, go to the places that make you come alive and feel happy & free, then you will attract the right person to you that way.

And all the same rules apply if you are dating as a single mother.
For all my single mothers out there, no matter how much you want to, you cannot make time stop. You have to get in the game as well. I don't care how many kids

you have everybody deserves love if they want it. And just, because you are a single mom, doesn't mean you only have to look for marriage from every man you meet. You have every right to enjoy the different experiences. Just make sure your kids are protected at all times. Babysitters, daycares, and friends and family who owe you favors exist for a reason. Be resourceful with your time and use it go out and get yours.

"OPEN YOUR EYES, LOOK WITHIN. ARE YOU SATISFIED WITH THE LIFE YOU ARE LIVING?

-BOB MARLEY

11

<u>Open Your Eyes</u>

Make connections and form relationships The more men you have on your radar the less stressful it will be. Before you get into the dating game you have to have experience. And the only way to gain experience is to get into the game. But that doesn't mean wait for a man to enter you have to take your self on dates. Finally, we have entered into the last part of the book. The good part of this whole ordeal because finding the right man to be in love with is so beautiful if you let it. You are going to learn how to get back in the game and how to enjoy the process of finding love.

So what's the point of know all this. Here is a thought. If you want to get over your ex you have to move on to the next. I come to realization that person you was so in love with wasn't because he was such a great person or else y'all would still be together. It more had to do with him being able to fill the void of feeling connected to some one. It honestly doesn't have to be him. It's not cause he was some great ducking person that u miss him. It was because u felt connected to him. So find someone else to get connected to. Am I oversimplifying this or what. Maybe the idea of being in love is some damn overrated. You can love so many people. Don't be stuck on one.

Don't under estimate the power of connection. Some of you don't need to be in relationships some of you just need some male friends to exchange some masculine energy with. And if it turn into love and infatuation more power to you

Knowing all this information is worthless if you don't do it. Go where the men are you can't be afraid to meet new men . Last pep talk of getting them in the game.

And don't forget to make friends first. Or better yet open your eyes to the men that are already around you. Don't ignore the men who you already have deep bonds with. Usually, it just takes a spark of chemistry between you two and the physical and sexual attraction will appear.

DON'T TAKE LIFE TOO SERIOUSLY, YOU'LL NEVER GET OUT ALIVE ANYWAY.

12

You Only Live Once

"Don't take life too seriously. After all none of us are getting out alive anyway.
-Jill Shalvis

You only live once so go out and get what's yours. Life is meant to be lived and experienced but being connected and enjoying the experience with someone else makes it a whole lot better.

I can take such a light-hearted approach to the dating game and life overall because I like to think of life as a big dream and God is the dreamer. We are all the projections of Gods dream, so we are all connected. We are living out Gods thoughts which have become our reality. And often we forget we are all just little spirit beings/pieces of consciousness just having a very brief human experience and soon we will have to go back to our source God. So don't take anything in life too seriously because when the game is over, we all go back in the box. God wants us to experience every aspect of this human being experience. From pain to love it was all created with Gods thoughts.

And since we are made in the likeness of God we have the power to change the course of this dream at any moment.

Just like when you have your own dream, the moment you become aware you are dreaming you can do anything you put your mind to. Like if you want to fly in a dream all you have to do is think it and then all of a sudden you start flying. So that's the same power you have in this reality.

The moment you wake up and become aware in this dream called life you have the ability to create anything you want. So stay woke my friends and enjoy this dream called life. You have the power.

by. Nancy Beauplan

Thank You!

by. Nancy Beauplan

by. Nancy Beauplan

ABOUT THE AUTHOR

Nancy M. Beauplan is on a mission to empower women to become fearless, fabulous & free. Her message to women is to "Don't Be Bitter, Get Better & Make Money" Her F*ckHim book series is geared to helping women get their life back on track after heartbreak so they can eliminate the unnecessary pain & suffering from their lives. You can find out more about her at www.nancybcreatives.com or shop her book collection at www.fvckhim.com or amazon.

Made in the USA
Middletown, DE
31 March 2017